Stude
Resou

GW01326065

BY DR

1

Tania Richards Photography

Dr Dominique Thompson is a GP, young people's mental health expert, TEDx speaker, author and educator, with over 20 years of clinical experience caring for students, most recently as Director of Service at the University of Bristol Students' Health Service. It was for this work that she was named Bristol Healthcare Professional of the Year 2017.

She is a clinical advisor for the Royal College of GPs, and for Student Minds, the UK's student mental health charity. She was the GP member of the NICE Eating Disorders' guidelines development group, and the Universities UK StepChange and Minding Our Future committees. Dominique is also a member of the UK Mental Wellbeing in Higher Education group (MWBHE).

Dominique's TEDx talk, "What I Learnt from 78,000 GP Consultations with University Students," highlights some of the causes behind the recent rise in young people's mental health distress, and suggests ways in which everyone can better support the younger generation.

You can follow her on Twitter @DrdomThompson and on Instagram as drdom99.

First published in Great Britain 2019 by Trigger

The Foundation Centre
Navigation House, 48 Millgate, Newark
Nottinghamshire NG24 4TS UK

www.triggerpublishing.com

British Library Cataloguing in Publication Data

A CIP catalogue record for this book is available upon
request from the British Library

ISBN: 978-1-78956-172-2

Dominique Thompson has asserted her right under the Copyright,
Design and Patents Act 1988 to be identified
as the author of this work

Cover design and typeset by Fusion Graphic Design Ltd

Printed and bound in Great Britain by Clays Ltd, Elcograf S.p.A

Paper from responsible sources

TRIGGER™

The mental health & wellbeing publisher

www.triggerpublishing.com

Thank you for purchasing this book.
You are making an incredible difference.

Proceeds from all Trigger books go directly to
The Shaw Mind Foundation, a global charity that focuses
entirely on mental health. To find out more about
The Shaw Mind Foundation, visit
www.shawmindfoundation.org

MISSION STATEMENT

Our goal is to make help and support available for every
single person in society, from all walks of life. We will
never stop offering hope. These are our promises.

Trigger and The Shaw Mind Foundation

the *Shaw* **mind**
FOUNDATION

Creating hope for children,
adults and families

To everyone who supports students – you are all heroes!
Thank you!

ROLE DEFINITIONS

A Who's Who of Student Support

GP (general practitioner)

A GP is a medically qualified doctor who sees people in the community, not in a hospital. They are able to help with all conditions, although they may have a special interest, for example in skin problems or mental health. They are sometimes called "family doctors", and will often refer patients to specialists, such as psychiatrists or psychologists, for specific problems.

Counsellor

A counsellor offers a safe, confidential space for individuals to talk. Counsellors help their clients explore their thoughts, feelings and actions to help them come to terms with life and find more hopeful and useful ways to approach their future. Counsellors will work in different ways depending on their training, but will always allow their client to take the lead in what they want to talk about. They do not offer advice, but through the empathic attention they give to their client's words, the client often discovers their own wisdom, helping them to lead a more fulfilling life.

Clinical Psychologist

A person who specialises in psychological or emotional conditions and mental health disorders. They will have specialised in the study of clinical psychology and will usually have a doctorate or PhD (though they're not medically qualified and will not able to prescribe medication). They assess people and diagnose mental health conditions or problems. They are trained in using talking and behavioural interventions specifically tailored to treat psychological disorders. They may use a range of therapy approaches which vary from psychodynamic to cognitive behavioural therapy, to family and couples' therapies, to interpersonal approaches. They base their assessment and treatment methods on scientific principles and outcomes, and will use the best evidenced method that helps to treat an individual.

Therapist

A term for professionals who use talking and behavioural therapies to support people with mental health conditions.

Psychiatrist

A medically qualified doctor who specialises in mental health conditions (also called psychiatric conditions) who can assess, make a diagnosis, offer advice, and prescribe medications. A psychiatrist is the only person who can prescribe some specialist medications. They work with GPs, therapists, psychologists and counsellors, and will usually recommend a type of talking or behavioural treatment.

CONTENTS

INTRODUCTION

Life is not straightforward.

There will always be challenges, difficult times, and bumps in the road, so being prepared and having a skills "toolkit" for coping with these obstacles is essential.

University in particular can be a tricky time, with academic pressure, deadlines and exams, occasional relationship and friendship conflicts, or financial issues likely to impact on you at some point.

Being ready for such potential problems – or at least knowing where to look for practical, relevant and reliable advice (and top tips!) if they occur – will ensure that they don't knock you off course for long. You will bounce back from any setbacks with the knowledge that you can deal with them, and you'll be even better prepared should things get tricky again.

This book is about learning those lifelong skills for bouncing back successfully.

Who is the book for?

This book is for any university student – or anyone preparing for uni – who wants a trustworthy source of advice and information. There will be signposting to additional resources on the way and an evidence-based approach to the skills described and recommended, grounded in solid research.

This book should be something to which you can turn for support, so that you can cope when the going gets tough and become increasingly independent and resourceful for the future.

When will the book be useful to you?

There will of course be plenty of times when life throws you a curveball and you will manage just fine. But sometimes situations, emotions and conflicts will arise for which you feel less well-prepared and have less psychological strength to deal with at that moment.

This book is for those times when you feel like a failure or an imposter, or fear you are letting people down, or simply for when you have no idea how to have that difficult conversation with someone. Whether it's money or study worries keeping you awake at night, this book can help.

The scenarios and real-life examples might not exactly match what you are experiencing, but hopefully there will be enough similarities for you to connect with them and apply the advice to your own situation.

This book will be useful to you at any time you are struggling at uni – just dip in and use what's helpful to you.

CHAPTER 1

WHY IS BEING A STUDENT SO STRESSFUL SOMETIMES?

It seems fair to say that young people today are under pressure like no previous generation. A whole variety of factors combine to create what can feel like a "pressure-cooker society", and it is therefore no surprise that more and more young people seem to be suffering from mental distress. Being aware of some of these pressures will allow you to counter their negative effects and harness any positive angles to enhance your wellbeing.

For example, having insight into any perfectionist traits you may have will allow you to gain some perspective and reassess what might actually be "good enough" sometimes.

21st-century pressures

Competitiveness

In today's world, even the fun stuff has become competitive. Often we see things that would normally be hobbies – baking cakes, photography, writing or singing and dancing – as a form of competition. We see this everywhere and it can feel relentless.

This seems particularly true in the university or college lecture hall or seminar room, with the pressure on students to excel or get a First in their degrees, rather than just a broad education. Sometimes students are then pressured to do post-grad studies or get another diploma. It's a never-ending race to the top and it is exhausting for young people.

How can you try to take back some control over the uber-competitiveness of life?

- **Be aware** of your over-competitiveness – this is the first step!
- Choose whether or not to engage in competitiveness and when.
- Decide whether or not to participate in competitive activities beyond the obvious academic / career / sport-related ones.
- If you organise events for other students, consider not making them competitive and instead organise something "just for fun".

Perfectionism

There seems to be a close correlation between the overly competitive nature of our society and the documented rise in perfectionism among young adults (Curran and Hill, 2017). This seems to have driven a **huge increase in the number of students with perfectionist traits** in the USA, Canada and the UK over the last 30 years.

With perfectionist traits being closely linked to several mental health conditions such as anxiety, depression, self-harm, eating disorders and obsessive-compulsive disorder, it starts to become apparent why GPs and student support professionals are seeing more students with these conditions.

In trying to keep up with everyone else, trying to be *the* best rather than simply doing *your* best, you may be (in some cases) making yourselves ill.

If you're interested, and have 10 minutes to spare, I even did a TEDx talk on this called "What I Learnt from 78,000 GP Consultations with University Students", which you can watch online (Thompson, 2018).

We will talk more about how to tackle perfectionism later on.

Social Media

The fact that social media can magnify these issues is fairly well recognised. Apps such as Facebook, Instagram or Snapchat can really pile on the pressure. Not only are students driving themselves harder than ever before, but now they're being monitored and "graded" 24 / 7 via their own social media channels. Sometimes people feel the need to constantly compare themselves using this medium. Social media in itself might not cause mental ill health in many cases, but it may make a difficult situation worse.

Real-life example

Emma was a second-year student living with four other girls, all of whom were high-achieving and studying veterinary sciences, medicine, or law. She felt more than able to keep up with them academically, but doubted herself constantly when it came to fashion and image. She couldn't decide what to wear, whereas they seemed to find looking good so easy and were always sharing pictures of themselves online with funny comments and hashtags. She dreaded posting anything in case she got negative comments or few likes – or, worst of all, no reaction at all. Emma knew she was bright, yet despite being at the university of her dreams, she never felt good enough, slim enough or cool enough if she looked at her social media feeds. The pressure was making her unhappy.

For some of you, social media *will* be the source of emotional distress (e.g. seeing traumatic events online), or it might make you feel worse by fuelling obsessive tendencies (driving the need for "likes" or followers) or by playing into body image insecurities.

You might want to think about how much you engage with social media if it's making you stressed, and try the following tips in order to reduce any negative impact it may have:

- **Think about how much you engage with social media** – are you using it too much?
- **Remember** that social media can be a source of support and useful resources if needed.
- **Choose to follow uplifting accounts** that don't make you feel inadequate.
- **Limit your time looking at it** by only having the apps on your laptop or computer and taking them off your phone.
- **Take active steps** to make time for activities and hobbies that don't require you to be online.

It's also important to:

- **Uninstall apps and / or avoid websites** that make you feel bad.
- **Remind yourself** that photos and videos are often heavily edited online to make people's lives look ideal. Try to avoid comparing yourself to what you see on your feed.
- **Keep in mind** that you can't always go to every social event or be part of every conversation, and that that doesn't mean that you're not still part of your friendship group (Edwards, 2019).

Meritocracy

This is a tough one. Culturally, we are encouraged to believe from a young age that if we work really hard and give things our best shot, then we will be appropriately *rewarded* with happiness, money, success, a nice place to live, a great relationship, and a happy family.

However, what this theory (that rewards are given based on merit / talent alone) fails to consider, and which can lead to us feeling like we have "failed" (because we really *did* try our very best and it was *apparently* not good enough), is that *many other variables* can affect the "rewards" that we receive. Let me give you an example.

You are going to a job interview. You have the right qualifications and the perfect outfit and you have practised for an infinite variety of questions, perfecting your best "engaged but not trying too hard" voice and tone. The interview goes well, you don't make any giant mistakes, and you leave thinking, "Nailed it!"

But here's the thing ... what you don't realise is that the lead interviewer's cat died that morning and no matter how you performed or what you did, it was never going to go well for you – or indeed, anyone else – that day.

And although the fellow interviewers tried to cheer their colleague up, it didn't work, and no one got that job.

There was nothing you could have done differently and you still don't know what went wrong, but the point is that *despite your best efforts* sometimes life won't work out as you expect it to.

Meritocracy can sometimes be a myth.

There are some great videos online by celebrities (Matthew McConaughey, Martin Lewis of MoneySavingExpert) illustrating this point, explaining how their success was probably talent driven, but also down to **luck, who you know, being in the right place at the right time, taking risks and so on**.

Just trying hard and doing your best (or even *being* the best) is not the *only* factor in success.

The message here is, therefore:

- To **do your best**, but to accept that there will sometimes be unknown factors at play.
- Take a pragmatic and realistic approach when things go "wrong". It will allow you to bounce back far more easily next time.
- Don't tear yourself up over the job you don't get, or the proposal that fails, or the exam you score poorly in.
- Think about what went well and look at what you might do differently in future, then use that next time in the knowledge that there will **always** be an unknown element in everything we do in life.
- Remember that from some of these "failures" will come your greatest opportunities.

Real-life example

Mila applied for a junior doctor's job in a hospital paediatric department, and of the six candidates, she was the only one not to be given one of the five posts.

She was naturally upset, but a few days later she saw a poster asking for doctors to join a 12-week expedition to Malaysia, which she would never have considered applying for if she hadn't had a period of unemployment now looming.

Mila went on the expedition, and 20 years later it remains one of the most fun, challenging, exciting and best experiences of her life. And it would never have happened if she had got that paediatric job!

Managing your parents and carers

The lives, expectations, personal problems and beliefs of your parents and carers all impact on you as a student, and perhaps in ways you never fully appreciated until you moved to uni.

Families can feel very invested in your life and future, and not just financially, of course.

They may feel that they have a *right* to be involved in the decisions you make and the path you take, and while sometimes they may have a point (after all, they might have helped to get you to this point to a greater or lesser extent), you may not be as keen to discuss all your decisions with them – or for them to be involved at all.

Real-life example

Ben was a 19-year-old first-year psychology student. He had been struggling with his sexual identity for a few years, had hoped that everything would be different once he was at uni, and that he would be able to finally tell his family he was gay. Unfortunately, things did not turn out that way. As the year progressed, he still felt unable to speak to his father about it, despite years of distress and previous bullying at school. His mum had died when he was 11 and he did not think that his dad would accept the fact that he was gay. After a few months he decided to speak to his tutor about his worries, as the tutor seemed relaxed and open about talking with the students. With the tutor's support, Ben was able to find a website with helpful advice and came up with a plan of how to broach the topic with his dad at a calm moment.

If you can, try to find a balance between allowing family to feel a part of your life to an extent that you are comfortable with, while retaining your autonomy and independence as you establish your own identity and future plans.

Unfortunately, conflict can arise not only as students develop personal lives that challenge a parent or carer's beliefs, but also if they make academic or career choices that the family feel disappointed or confused by. For example, your parents may always have hoped you would become a lawyer, architect or pharmacist, but you want to study languages or write for a living.

Remember:

- It's *your* life and you should absolutely follow the path that will bring you fulfilment and happiness
- But it might be thoughtful to **take the time to talk to your family** about your views and choices so that they feel involved and considered in the process.

This may be especially important to do if they are struggling with your decisions or you need to have a difficult conversation (see later for how to approach these).

Talking to family and friends can be difficult

GPs are very understanding and aware of the fact that not everyone feels able to talk to their family and friends about any worries they may have, whether academic (they fear letting people down), financial (they fear being a burden, or that they will be criticised), mental health-related (they fear being stigmatised or dismissed as "making a fuss"), or relationship-related (they worry that they won't be taken seriously or, if sexual identity is the issue, that others will be unsupportive at best, or cut them off at worst).

Talking to your closest friends and family can be challenging, but it is essential to at least consider it and try to involve them and gain their support if you can, because we all need support from other people in our lives, and they would likely be keen to help if possible.

You might even want to take them to a GP appointment with you, just to set the scene for them and ensure that everyone understands what is happening, if that feels relevant and helpful.

Talking to them about your worries or changes you plan to make in your life won't always make everyone happy, but at least you will have been true to yourself while being considerate of their desire to be part of the process.

In summary

All of these different 21st-century pressures and demands can really build up at a time of transition and academic expectation, so be kind to yourself. Take the time to think about the challenges, and consider how to respond or react for the best outcome.

In the next few chapters, we will consider the most common problems worrying students, what some real-life examples might look like, and which possible solutions or strategies you might use to deal with them.

CHAPTER 2

PEOPLE PROBLEMS

Relationship ups and downs are a part of life, and learning to recognise when things are going wrong and how to address them is a skill that takes time to learn. It isn't always easy to get right. Some people will always find it difficult to address this sort of interpersonal discord in their lives, but hopefully some of the tips below will help you to think about those situations that are stressing you and give you some ideas of what to do about them.

1. Conflict in friendships / relationships / with flatmates

There is no doubt that a significant amount of the distress caused to students at university is from conflict in relationships with others, whether it be from making new friends, leaving old friends behind (or finding that people you wish you had left behind have turned up at uni with you!), or learning to live with strangers from around the world. Perhaps issues arise in communicating with romantic partners (or those you *hope* will be intimate partners!), and the recurring nightmare of group relationships, which can be destabilised by individuals or cliques (this can be in relation to living arrangements, group work on your course, or friendship groups).

This might include dealing with:

- Slovenly flatmates
- Cheating partners
- Unkind or unthoughtful friends
- Overbearing parents
- Irritable or demanding academic staff

More worryingly, it might also include aggressive partners, risky behaviour by others that impacts on you, and even violence or assault in some (rare) cases. If these scenarios are happening in your life or your friends' lives, you will need professional support and advice, so don't hesitate to ask for help. Plenty will be available.

Real-life example

Ted, Andy, Beth and Saira were living together in their third year and got along pretty well. Then Beth met Richard, and the two of them started spending a lot of time together. Richard seemed to be at the flat more and more often. He shared their food, used their bathroom, slept over, and soon it seemed like there were five flatmates, but only four of them were paying the bills and buying the food. Nobody wanted to say anything initially, but eventually Saira mentioned it to the boys and they agreed that it was irritating all of them. They liked Richard, and were happy for Beth, but this was stretching their patience. They decided to have a "difficult conversation".

For many scenarios, the following skills may be a good place to start.

How to have "difficult conversations" or basic conflict-resolution skills

These skills might prove useful throughout your life!

Avoiding conflict or difficult situations may seem like the easier option sometimes, and we all do it, but it might be that the best path to take is the one that is tricky now, and it will hopefully lead you to a better long-term end result.

Remember that (in general):

- People want to be understood, listened to, and heard. Start with this in mind when you are having a difficult conversation.
- People might feel threatened or become very emotional.
- There may be stuff going on for them that you are not aware of, whether or not they choose to share that with you.
- There are always two sides to every story; even if you strongly believe your side to be the most morally or ethically right, there may be additional factors that you are not yet aware of.
- We all occasionally have to get **comfortable with being uncomfortable** – in this case, living with a non-ideal situation. Remember, everything is a phase (more on this later). It's temporary and will be over soon. In the meantime, focus on what matters most to you, smile, and keep going!

TOP TIPS:

- Pick a good time, not when people are just going out / coming in, exhausted or caught unawares. Mention that you'd like to talk and agree a time that suits you both.
- Be compassionate, whenever possible.

- Listen *actively*; hear what they are *really* saying. Read their body language too.
- Try to avoid aggressive language / swearing and so on, as it really raises the stress levels and rarely achieves anything helpful.
- Communicate clearly what you are trying to say and perhaps plan the **three key points** you want to make in advance.
- Be prepared to compromise or agree on something slightly less than ideal in order to resolve the situation. It might not be perfect, but you should feel able to live with the decisions made.
- Sometimes it is impossible to sort a problem out or agree on a solution, in which case you might need to let that one go and **agree to disagree** in order to move on with your lives.

If the feelings from conflict or difficult relationships are overwhelming

Some people are particularly sensitive to conflict with others, and take perceived slights and criticisms very badly – perhaps even out of proportion – or they can misread communications from friends or partners, leading them to **feel extremely distressed or even to harm themselves**.

If you recognise this reaction in yourself it may be helpful to talk to a healthcare professional like a GP, psychologist, or counsellor about it, as you might find that learning specific skills through therapy may be useful for future relationships.

In the immediate aftermath of self-harm there is support available from organisations such as Samaritans, or online website or apps designed to help you (see our list of resources at end of book).

This is not just a "young person thing" either; I have spoken to several academics and university staff over the years who have suffered with these feelings and self-harmed. The important thing for their recovery has been their ability to seek help and professional therapy, though sometimes it has taken them years to do so. They all say they wish they had got help sooner.

2. Difficulty making friends or meeting new people

It's not uncommon for students to book a GP appointment because they "don't have any friends". It's always quite saddening, and GPs often wish that they could prescribe social activities to help them meet like-minded people to make new connections.

In some ways, of course, universities *do* provide a variety of opportunities to meet new people, but it can be particularly challenging to do this if you have Asperger's syndrome (autism spectrum disorder) or social anxiety, for example.

Many people from all sorts of backgrounds and cultures can struggle to connect with others, but the wonderful thing about arriving at a new place is that there are literally thousands of people all looking to make new friends, learn new things and try new experiences.

Why does having friends matter?

Social connectedness is recognised as a really great way to stay healthy and mentally strong (Jose, Ryan and Prior, 2012), so even if you quite like your own company, it may be good for you to connect with other people occasionally. Feeling a sense of belonging, of being linked to others and having a role, helps us to stay well and find our purpose in life.

In other words, people who are well-connected to others socially have been shown to have greater wellbeing in life.

Whether at home, at school, at uni, at work, or in the community, it is well worth finding some other people you enjoy spending time with.

So, let's have a think about how you might make some new connections.

TOP TIPS

Not everyone finds it easy to connect with others, so here are some tips that might help!

- **Get out there!** Say yes to invitations to meet up, to charity fundraising, to sporting events, to gigs. Try them and see if there's anyone there who sees life like you do. It doesn't have to be a proper invitation either; just seeing an advert for them is fine. Show up and see what happens! The key is to get out of your room!

- **Use social media** to find out about events etc., but don't use it instead of actually seeing people face to face. Having friends online is fine, but should not replace the very real human need to have friends in person too. Once you have connected with people online you may want to meet up with them later on.

- **Smile!** It's a wonderful way to break the ice and make you seem like a nice person who others would like to speak to and be friends with. Similarly, say hello in corridors, even to strangers. It doesn't have to be weird; just a quick 'Hi!' and a brief smile is a start, and people will subconsciously file you in the "Good People" category of their brain.

- If you have **Asperger's or other specific challenges**, then check in with your university support teams, who often organise get-togethers that are sensitive to particular needs. They will know which other local organisations hold events or gatherings in the area, like a quiet pub meet-up, or quiz night and pizza, if that's what you prefer. It doesn't have to include alcohol!

- Join societies that provide the activities you enjoy (or even try a completely new one) – whether it's politics, quidditch, crochet or baking, there seems to be something for everyone!

- Join the student radio or newspaper teams; you can just help out, make tea, suggest ideas and be in the background initially, if you're shy.
- **Volunteer!** This is an amazing way to meet new people, who are very likely to be friendly, kind, and compassionate. And you will be helping others too, which is always a bonus! Check out local volunteering opportunities online or via your Students' Union.
- Read articles like "The Science of Making Friends as an Adult" by Vanessa Van Edwards, which explains how we can connect with others without coming over as too needy or weird.

Real-life example

Arjun had always been shy. He'd had a close group of friends at school, but found he was struggling to meet people at uni. Everyone seemed so confident and bubbly. It was a bit unnerving. The first few weeks passed, and although he was going to lectures and people were friendly enough, he hadn't really made any good friends yet. He called home after a month and mentioned it to his mum. She was naturally concerned for him, but suggested that he volunteer through the Students' Union, initially to get out and about and see his new city a bit more, but also to meet some like-minded people. She also suggested the chess club at the SU, and the martial arts' societies, since he had enjoyed it at school.

He had been reluctant to go along on his own, but with his mum's encouragement and a 'What's the worst that could happen?' ringing in his ears, he followed both of her suggestions in the next week. He even discovered a martial art that he'd never heard of before, and over the next few weeks and months he gradually made a core group of three or four good new friends with whom he could spend time.

3. Peer pressure

When you arrive at a new university, it is usual to want to try to fit in, settle down and feel like part of the crowd.

Many students then find that they feel pressured to participate in activities such as drinking alcohol, taking drugs (including study drugs) or having sex when they don't feel comfortable or ready to do so. They worry that if they don't join in, if they say no or are seen to be the odd one out, that they will be ostracised, isolated, mocked, or cut out of the friendship group.

Obviously, none of those options are appealing when you have just arrived somewhere new!

The reality is that fewer young people are drinking and using drugs.

It may be helpful to know that recent figures show that an increasing number of students (one in five, according to the UK National Union of Students, 2018) are "teetotal" (choosing not to drink alcohol at all), and fewer young people than before are using drugs (six out of ten students, according to a survey by the UK Higher Education Policy Institute (HEPI) in 2018, had *never* used drugs).

In other words, if you choose to be moderate or careful in your approach, you will **not** be alone. So how can you say no in a way in which doesn't make you feel uncomfortable? There are a number of options you can try.

TOP TIPS:

- Respond with a clear, 'No thank you.'
- If you feel you can't do this, give another reason or even a small white lie (such as 'I'm on antibiotics' or 'I get migraines').
- Make a joke to diffuse the pressure.
- Get a friend to back you up if there's any resistance.
- Suggest an alternative activity.
- If all else fails, you can make your excuses and leave ('I'm feeling ill / tired / sick' / 'I've got an early lecture' and so on).

Remember, genuine friends will never push or force you to do things you don't want to do, so if there is continued pressure, it may be time to find new friends too.

4. Dealing with moral dilemmas or difficult decisions about life

Uni life is a time of change and looking to the future and can be filled with all sorts of difficult decisions – where to live, where to look for work after uni, whether to study after your course finishes and so on ...

Moral dilemmas may also arise where you just don't know what to do. Your course-mate's partner makes a move on you, for example – do you tell your friend?

TOP TIPS:

- Write a list of pros and cons to each.
- Talk issues through with others who you trust.

- Another handy technique is **to have a conversation with yourself.**

The latter technique is where you talk things through in your head, rationalising or arguing them out with yourself. You could perhaps even unleash your inner four-year-old and ask yourself "Why?" a lot, in order to reflect on how a situation is making you feel in general.

This can be great if you're wrestling with a moral dilemma or a problem in your life, such as whether or not to tell your flatmate that you saw her partner kissing someone else last night (this seems to happen a lot!).

Try This:

Me: Hmm, I don't think I should see John anymore.

Also me: But if I dump him, I'll be alone forever and have no one to hang out with when everyone else is all paired up! Why would I do that?

Me: But he's making me stressed and unhappy when he doesn't do what he says he'll do, like be on time, call me, message me, and come out with my friends when he said he would.

Me: But those are small things; it's not like he's aggressive or mean, so why am I being so picky?!

Me: But it shows he doesn't respect me! He doesn't value my time and he's being careless with my feelings.

Me: But I'll be alone!

Me: Better to be alone for a while than with someone who doesn't really care about me. Okay. Maybe I'll talk to him about how I'm feeling, and see if he is keen to make more of an effort and do as he promises; that's a good place to start ...

As a technique it can also be useful if you are alone, either at home or abroad, with no one immediately available to take the other side of the conversation. So, for example, "shall I take that intern role? They're not offering a salary but the experience would be amazing ... but I need the money too." And so on.

Such techniques are actually recommended by psychologists to help us think things through and avoid making rash decisions. We need to ask ourselves awkward questions like "Why am I finding this difficult?" in order to process feelings, and even to consolidate learning, which as students can be really practical.

So, the next time you are having a dilemma or feel like you're in a tight spot, try having a conversation with yourself and calmly think through what's going on for you at that moment.

CHAPTER 3

HEALTH PROBLEMS

1. Mental health

The current generation of students is much better educated about mental health and wellbeing, and is much less likely to stigmatise either themselves or others than previous generations.

Having said that, there can still be real barriers preventing people from getting the help they need. These could be concerns about what others will think, the potential effect on vocational courses and "Fitness to Practise", or simply not realising that there is a health problem in the first place. This can lead to significant difficulty accessing the care required when people do seek help (because of waiting lists and so on).

The current wave of students seems to be experiencing more mental distress than previous generations, and much has been said about why that might be, so if you are worried about your own mental health or that of a close friend, then don't hesitate to discuss your concerns with a professional.

TOP TIPS:

- The university will have multiple services set up to support students, so if you're not sure where to start, check the uni website or ask your academic department staff / tutor for guidance about where to go.
- Look up "Student Support Services". Your residential / accommodation teams will also know where to signpost you to.
- The key is not to hide away and suffer in silence, but to talk to someone in a position to help you, such as a GP, psychologist or counsellor, and start the conversation. Whether it's about your own wellbeing or that of a friend, they will have dealt with such issues hundreds of times before. The reason they work in a university in the first place is usually because they want to support students, so please do approach them.

A word about carer students (in particular, students who care for other students)

Many students also support other students, and some become carers for their partners, or flatmates. This can place a huge pressure on the carer student at a time when they have many other pressures to balance, as well as potentially leading them to develop a mental health condition too.

The support provided can vary from looking after a flatmate's antidepressant medication to ensure that they don't take too many, to constantly accompanying them to classes, appointments and activities. It can be exhausting, but students can be incredibly generous and self-sacrificing without realising the potential negative impact it may then have on their own wellbeing.

If this is you, then there may be lots of support available at your university for carers, so do ask either the GP practice, counselling service, or other student support teams what's available to help you – and, of course, to support the student you are caring for.

2. Food and healthy eating

It can be surprisingly tricky to eat well and healthily at uni. Whether the catered food is not to your taste, or self-catering means that you let the food shopping slide to focus on your essay, or that you exist on takeaways for weeks at a time through exam season, getting your vitamins, fibre and "brain food" can prove complicated. Anxiety and stress can also have bad effects on your guts.

Lots of students go to see the GP with constipation, irritable bowel syndrome (IBS), or related bowel symptoms, and often all that is needed is a bit of time spent thinking about some better food choices: the right kind of fibre, eating something that "doesn't have a label on it" (i.e. it's fresh and not out of a packet or shop-bought / ready-made), and drinking enough water (staying well hydrated).

TOP TIPS:

Healthy eating: don't wing it, plan it!

There are various ways to achieve a healthy student diet, such as:

- Planning shopping deliveries
- Buying and using simple cook books
- Joining culinary Students' Union societies
- Keeping fruit in your room (and actually eating it, not just using it as an ornament!)
- Sharing a cooking rota with flatmates
- Cooking in bulk at weekends then freezing it for the week ahead
- Planning your budget

But the key is to *actively* think about it. Spend some time planning ahead and setting things in place, then get on with other things, knowing that the food / recipe shopping / rota / extra vitamins are taken care of.

If you are having possible stress-related bowel symptoms (irregular bowel habit, bloating, wind and tummy pains), a simple strategy may be to try a FODMAP diet initially (designed for irritable bowel syndrome-specific relief, see resources at end of book) and see if that helps. If things aren't any better after four weeks, then please see a GP. If you are worried about your symptoms, then definitely don't ignore them. Get yourself checked out by a nurse or doctor!

It is worth remembering that eating issues or eating disorders can start – or get worse – at university, often because eating patterns can become chaotic or because stress levels rise. So if you are worried about your eating, or even not sure what's going on with your food and eating behaviours, then seek advice and support early. Don't wait for things to deteriorate.

3. Some advice about sleep

We all underestimate the importance of sleep, and yet the best-selling book *Why We Sleep* by Matthew Walker has, in the words of one reviewer, shown "how a good night's shut-eye can make us cleverer, more attractive, slimmer, happier, healthier and ward off cancer … it's probably a little too soon to tell you that it saved my life, but it's been an eye opener" (Mark O'Connell, Guardian).

Missing out on sleep, the book says, can have a catastrophic effect on our health and wellbeing.

GPs often tell students that rather than resorting to study drugs, as many do in order to stay awake and work longer, they would be better off getting a good night's sleep and then having a cup of coffee in the morning if they need it.

If you want to learn more about how sleep makes us better at learning and remembering things, you might also like to watch Russell Foster's brilliant TEDx talk on *Why Do We Sleep*.

So, how do we get a good night's sleep?

Well, first of all, before we get into the "sleep rules" it's important to understand that sleep is a *habit*, and so if it has been "broken" and you are not sleeping well, or if you have been sleeping in the day and staying up all night, then it will take time to reset your biological clock and get into a good habit.

About six weeks of following the sleep rules should do it, but if you're still struggling after that, talk to a doctor or therapist about it. Don't suffer in silence.

Insomnia and disrupted sleep patterns can be absolute torture. Rest assured, most GPs still remember the horror of junior doctor life, going for days without sleep, or working nights for long stretches, so they'll have every sympathy! Please do not ignore this essential wellbeing function, especially as it helps improve the quality of your academic work, as well as keeping you healthy.

The "Sleep Rules"

- Try to go to bed and get up at the same time every day, Monday to Sunday. Use your alarm if necessary, to set the routine!
- Try to be asleep when it's dark and awake when it's light – but within reason; midnight to 8.00am, for example. Don't sleep in the day time or stay up all night to work; you need **about eight to nine hours sleep a night** as a young adult.
- If you have to nap in the day, then do it before 3.00pm.
- Stop all work and turn off all screens at least **one hour** before bedtime.

- Spend that hour winding down, chatting with a friend, listening to quiet music, having a warm bath, reading quietly, or watching TV (nothing too scary or exciting!).
- Exercise in the daytime before about 6.00pm, and don't have caffeine or alcohol late in the evening, nor should you eat any heavy meals (although light snacks are ok).
- Create a gadget-free zone. That means no lights that might blink at night, no notifications lighting up the room, and no clocks that you can stare at when you should be sleeping.
- Don't lie in bed awake for hours. If you can't get to sleep, get up, do a relaxing activity for a while, and, when you feel sleepier, try to get back to sleep. (medlineplus.gov)

Stick to these rules for about four to six weeks, and if that isn't working then check out Cognitive Behavioural Therapy for Insomnia (CBT-I), which is proven to improve sleep, as well as making time to talk to a professional about how you are doing, as there may be other things you can try that can help to improve your sleep and mood.

4. Returning to studies after absence

Many students (at all levels of study) have to take time out for ill health (mental or physical), family issues, bereavements, pregnancy, and sometimes because they have lost all motivation and need a leave of absence in order to regroup and regain their perspective on life. It is probably fair to say that not enough students take a leave of absence when they need to, and that more might benefit from making the most of the university systems in place to help them take a break when it becomes necessary.

Most of these students return to higher education after their break feeling well refreshed and recovered, and with renewed enthusiasm for their studies, but it can occasionally be tricky to settle back into student life. This might be because they have experienced a different pace of life in which they have had more or less freedom, or they have a new health condition to manage, their friends have all moved on to the year above or have graduated, or simply because of changes in the university environment.

TOP TIPS:

Adjustment to any change takes time and can be difficult, so it may help to prepare for a return to your studies by:

- Communicating in advance with people with whom you might socialise or live with upon your return.
- Contacting your academic tutors to ensure that you have any reading lists or to get ideas about what to study in advance.
- Considering a "back-to-uni" day or weekend visit in order to physically experience the campus / housing options, and check out any alterations or unforeseen changes on campus that might otherwise trip you up emotionally.
- If you are going to need medical care or psychological therapy, then it can be helpful to liaise with the GP team or counselling service in advance of your return and set the appointments up ready for your arrival.
- All universities have Access or Disability units, so you might like to contact them and see what they might be able to offer you in order to ease your transition back into university life. You won't know until you ask!

With some preparation and planning, a return to studying should be smooth and relatively uneventful, but it can help to adjust expectations prior to returning, as life may be a little different (in both good and less good ways) on settling back in.

CHAPTER 4

ACADEMIC PROBLEMS

1. Academic pressure

Academic work is undoubtedly one of the greatest burdens felt by students.

The regular assessments; the competition with highly competent peers in the subject (i.e. you are no longer near the top of the class perhaps); the overt competition and discussion of exam questions, results, and grades by other students; the feeling that you are investing so much energy, time and possibly money in your degree or studies so you can't risk failing; the expectations of parents ... All of these are genuine pressures than can potentially create enormous strain throughout your time at university.

TOP TIPS:

There are several ways to manage academic stress and ensure that you don't let it overwhelm you:

- You can check out academic skills workshops and learn about the most effective ways to study and learn.
- You can ensure that you have a good work-life balance and care for yourself properly throughout your time at university. This may include following the "5 Ways to

Wellbeing" (Connect, Be Active, Take Notice, Keep Learning and Give, Mind 2019) or checking out some self-care tips such as blocking time off to relax, see friends or exercise.

- You can ask for academic support from university staff, who are there to help you and ensure you reach your academic potential (it's literally their job!).

- And if you are struggling, **then don't ignore it**. Talk to the student support services and flag the problem up before it becomes a crisis.

Academic pressure can be high risk

There are many things that stress students out, but academic pressure is one of the greatest concerns. It has been shown to be linked to a heightened risk of suicide in young people under 20 (NCISH, 2017), and in students specifically it has been shown that suicide may be associated with exam times at university (peaking in January and April) (NCISH, 2018).

So if you're feeling the strain, please don't keep pushing on, crushed under the weight of your degree. Talk to someone and let them help you to lighten that load. You're not alone, and help is available. You are not letting anyone down and it is not "failure", we all need help sometimes.

Real-life example

Roshni was a 23-year-old international student, studying for a Master's'. Her tutor had noted that she looked dishevelled and was very quiet in seminars, so they encouraged her to have a chat.

Roshni said that she had been feeling low for months, but her parents "didn't believe in mental health" so she had not felt able to speak to them. She did not feel comfortable talking to her flatmates about herself, and didn't have many friends at the university.

Academically, she was worried about a presentation which was coming up. She asked her tutor for help, and they were happy to listen.

The tutor was very supportive and compassionate. They sat with her as she made a GP appointment to discuss her low mood, reassured her about the presentation, and talked about how she could gain confidence in her academic work by going to some skills groups being run in the department. They told her that she was not alone and that they would meet with her each week. She felt happier and much reassured by these first steps to getting back on track.

2. Procrastination

Have you tidied your room for the fifth time, put all your books in alphabetical order, then colour-coordinated your sock drawer? Have you doodled, made lists, and updated all your social media accounts? Have you slept till you can't sleep anymore? Do you recognise yourself in the wheel of suffering (right)?

Then you, my friend, are definitely procrastinating!

We all do it. Staring at a blank screen or page, not knowing where to start with an essay, having "writer's block", feeling like you have to read *everything* about a topic before you can start writing about it or designing your project ... There are so many ways to feel defeated before you've even started your work.

Procrastination is a **very** common problem at university, whether you're a student or an academic. On the plus side, because it is such a well-recognised issue, entire workshops and skills classes are run in most universities to help you get back on track, so definitely check out what is available where you are, and sign up for one.

Do you recognise yourself in the Procrastination Wheel of Suffering?

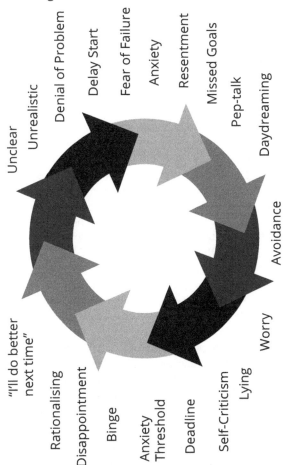

With kind permission to reproduce by Dr David Rasch.

Top Tips to Battle Procrastination

Here are a few tips to get you started while you book yourself into a procrastination / academic skills / writing masterclass (with thanks to Abby Shovlin, and Rasch, 2018):

1. Start writing **something** – anything. Start in the middle, write a paragraph, go back to the beginning, write the ending – it doesn't matter; just write **something**. Even if that all gets lost / deleted in the final draft, you have to start somewhere.

2. Remember that nobody ever writes the final draft straight off. Your essay / project / idea / thesis will **evolve**. The final draft may look nothing like your first draft!

3. It takes time, but start with something on the page in front of you. It doesn't need to be perfect, or even relevant to the final product. Seeing something written in front of you will then allow you to think about it **outside of your head** and critique it or expand upon it. This **"brain dump"** can then lead to analysis and planning.

4. Write an **"elevator pitch"** of your idea – that is to say, see if you can summarise what you're trying to do in one or two sentences. Then expand on it. (Use mind maps if they help here.)

5. Learn about **Active Reading**. This skill can be very useful for analysing what you read, asking questions of the text as you go along, then thinking about how what you have just read could be interpreted or useful for what you want to produce, write or create (www2.open. ac.uk, 2018).

A word about "Going Blank in Exams"

This is quite common, and happens when you suddenly feel really anxious about the exam. There are a few things you can do to **reduce the likelihood of the mind blank** happening in the first place, and also to manage them if they do.

1. **Getting a good night's sleep.** Sleeping well before exams is sometimes tricky, but a good night's sleep *after* a day of revising actually helps to consolidate all your learning and seal those facts into your memory, so making sure that you get your eight or nine hours of shut-eye is key throughout your revision.

2. **Revising in a variety of locations** means that when you are then in the *exam* location, you are less put off by the new environment. So make sure you revise in the different libraries, the department, at home and so on, keeping your brain on its toes by changing your surroundings regularly (Carey, 2015).

3. Equally, revise in situations that are **not** all peaceful and relaxing in order to prepare yourself for the anxiety and stress scenario of the exam. Get used to working where there are occasional noises or activity around you, so that you train your brain into focusing **despite these distractions**. It doesn't need to be a combat zone, just not always a library!

4. Learn some **relaxation techniques** such as mindfulness, or just good old-fashioned breathing exercises in order to bring your anxiety under control and overcome the mind blank.

Top tips for general exam preparation

- Don't leave it all till the last minute: plan your revision and stick to that plan.
- Use flow charts, diagrams and images – we learn brilliantly when we use visual aids!
- Practice old exam papers and questions.

- Explain topics to people who don't study them with you (or to your family), as having to explain something helps us to understand it better.

- Take breaks for at least 10 minutes at a time. Stretch, walk around, or get outside and get some vitamin D.

- Eat sensible, healthy food, and stay hydrated. And don't skip breakfast on the day of the exam!

- Plan for the day of the exam: note down where it is, timings etc. (Yes, GPs have been asked for a note by someone who missed their exam because they "got lost on the way", and no, they don't write one!)

- Don't just copy out your lecture notes; read them, then write down what you remember for better long-term recall.

- If you like studying with others, work in a group and explain things to each other.

3. Lack of motivation / energy for work

Getting started on something can be hard enough when you have some ideas and enjoy your subject, but when students feel unmotivated, exhausted, lacking in energy or enthusiasm, then it can be near-impossible to get anything done.

It is not uncommon for students to seek help and advice from healthcare and support professionals for lack of motivation and apathy.

It can, of course, be part of a bigger problem such as **depression**. So, if you also have lost interest in doing the things you used to enjoy, and feel flat or down, or have poor sleep etc. for more than a week or two, then you must definitely seek advice, preferably from a GP initially.

And we mustn't forget that some medical conditions such as an **underactive** thyroid can also cause issues with energy levels and motivation, so that might need a check-up too.

TOP TIPS:

If those possible causes have been ruled out, and this is more about your studies and course itself (you hate it, the topic is dull, you didn't want to study it in the first place, it was a clearing option, your parents wanted you to do that subject etc.), then it may be helpful to **speak to someone in the university's careers department, or to an academic advisor**, for whom these issues make up a significant part of their daily workload.

There may be options you had not considered before or realised were even possible, such as:

- Trying a new or different module
- Changing courses
- Exploring opportunities to travel abroad
- In some cases, considering a change of university if necessary

You just need to ask for guidance and talk to the professionals about the problem you are having. After all, helping students to successfully complete a degree they enjoy and achieve their potential is literally their day job!

Try This:

Take a moment to **remember why you are doing what you are doing, and try to visualise what life might be like when it's done**.

Visualisation is a technique that some people find useful for focusing on a positive future scenario, instead of focusing on things that are not going well or are frustrating. Having a mental image of where you want to be or what you want to achieve can be a powerful way to help you get there, but you have to act on it too. If you are feeling stressed and need to remind yourself why you are doing what you are doing with all the effort it entails, visualisation allows you a moment to breathe and refocus.

Top Tips for Visualisation:

- Make sure you are in the right frame of mind, calm and ready to focus.
- Take time to build an image or vision of what life might look like, where you might be, what you might be doing, if things went well and worked out. It might be you walking up to collect your degree, it might be you in a great job, or travelling somewhere exciting because of your degree ...
- Ask yourself: what would have to be different and what might need to change to get you there?
- Try to feel excited or positive emotions about what you are imagining.
- Don't rush, enjoy the images and let yourself believe you can achieve these things.
- Keep visualising at different times – practice visualising to keep yourself on track and motivated.

Remember!

Universities exist (mainly) to educate people and award degrees – they want (and need!) you to be successful and happy with your course. So, engage with the staff to make sure you are!

CHAPTER 5

CONFIDENCE AND SELF-ESTEEM PROBLEMS

1. Perfectionism

Voltaire is often slightly misquoted as having written "Perfect is the enemy of good".

But take a moment to think about what he was saying. What he meant was that when we strive for perfection, we lose sight of (or ignore) what is "good" and "good enough". We can exhaust ourselves trying to be the best and making everything perfect when we could have achieved enjoyment and satisfaction with our activity / work by making it good enough.

In a world where perfectionism is on the increase (see previous section on 21st-century pressures), it can be very hard to maintain a perspective on what is **good enough**. But being able to accept "good enough" might actually be what saves your sanity and keeps you healthy.

If you work hard on something, give it your best effort and are pleased with what you have achieved, then try not to be derailed by others talking about their work, or their exam answers, or their projects, which can then lead you to feeling as though you should have done something differently.

Don't let them shake your confidence, and don't let their competitiveness drive you towards perfectionism. Learn when to stop working, and be pragmatic and say "That's enough, I've given it my best shot, and I'm ok with that."

What does perfectionism look like?

- Are you the person who gets 95% in a test and spends hours wondering what happened to the other 5%?
- Do you berate yourself for not getting top marks in a test, when in fact it was all new content and really tough for everyone?
- Are you highly self-critical if you don't come top, or if you don't consider your work to be perfect? Are you quite often late to hand work in because you are redoing it or still trying to make it perfect?
- Do you see your work only in extremes, either "perfect" or "the worst"?
- Do you aim for perfection from the beginning of a piece of work, and so delay, procrastinate and faff about because it's not perfect immediately?

This is what perfectionist traits look like. They can be highly destructive and negative for your wellbeing, as you can sometimes undermine yourself with your negative self-perception.

Perfectionism can lead to students either **avoiding** the work or activity completely, or **overcompensation** (such as feeling that you need to check your work six times, otherwise you will make a mistake and everyone will judge you).

Real-life example

Zack was a very creative humanities student. He only had a few weeks to go till his final essay was due to be handed in. He had started it, deleted it and restarted it countless times. He was never happy with his writing, and was angry with himself for "failing" at this task, as he viewed it. He wanted his last essay to be perfect, to blow people away, be original, and outstanding.

Zack knew he could do something special, but he was never satisfied with what he drafted. He kept telling himself that he was "rubbish" for not being able to craft a beautiful essay, and that he didn't deserve his degree if he couldn't do this properly. He was late handing in his essay as he procrastinated and struggled so much to complete the work.

If you recognise yourself and your behaviour in this or your perfectionist tendencies are having a negative impact on you, read on to find out more about techniques you can try straightaway.

TOP TIPS:

• Ask if there are workshops or help available for perfectionism at your university

It's becoming an increasing challenge for university communities and more and more support is being provided. There are specific CBT-related techniques that can help to break the cycle, too, so check to see if you can find help that includes these.

• Exercise self-compassion

This does **not** mean self-pity or self-indulgence.

Self-compassion is a concept whereby you are as kind and caring to yourself as you are to a good friend (Neff, 2018).

You don't need to suffer, push on through, or have a stiff upper lip. You can:

- Take the time to be kind to yourself
- Recognise that you are struggling and look after your own feelings

- Keep doing the things you want to be doing to ensure that you can function and feel well
- Make an active effort to stop criticising yourself

Human beings are not perfect; it's one of our most endearing traits. So embrace your imperfections and unique qualities.

Continuum technique

This technique involves adjusting what you consider to be "good enough", from "perfection" to "acceptable" or "good". Currently, you only consider *perfection* to be good enough, so we need to dial that down to what is **actually** good enough.

Start by aiming to complete a draft of the work which is "good enough". If you then have some time before the deadline, work on it in small chunks, improving sections bit by bit. If time runs out, you can hand it in – even though it may not be perfect, it will be good enough and on time!

This approach reduces pressure on you, and also reduces the risk of procrastination.

You can design your own continuum (using the diagram as an example) depending on your type of work or study, but the process will help you to agree with yourself what would be "good enough". See the diagram for more info.

You can then let go of unrealistic expectations (the far-right end of the continuum line).

"Good enough" might be getting *65%* not 85%, or writing about a topic that inspires and interests you but that you don't have time to read *everything* about (but you have read enough to be able to say something genuinely engaged and enthusiastic (and maybe even original!)). Try to think what "doing okay" would look like for you.

When you can find "good enough", you will have a lot more peace (and time!) in your life, but it can take time to adjust.

The Continuum technique – finding "good enough"

Aim Here

Aim Here

The worst	Below Average	Good enough Acceptable	Excellence	Perfection
To not hand anything in To not try	To hand in something incomplete	To hand in something that answers most of the question, and meets deadline	To hand in something that answers the whole question, is within the word count, and some parts flow well	To hand in something that answers every criteria, every sentence flows well, ideas are unique, beyond level of references required, covers every angle of the topic, within word count, 100% academic language, meets deadline

With kind permission to reproduce by Dr Emma Kerr of University of Newcastle, Australia.

2. Fear of failure / making mistakes

Closely linked to perfectionism is the fear of making mistakes or "failing".

Students are often very worried about being seen to "fail", even though what *they* view as "failure" may actually be a relatively straightforward, common or understandable mistake, *not* a disaster.

They can dread **feedback**, even though this is essential for all of us to improve in life and achieve what we want to achieve, such as a good degree, a great project, an innovative approach to an old problem in a PhD, and so on.

Young people are also often terrified of **letting other people down** – their parents, families, carers, friends, and sometimes tutors or teachers too. They worry about what others will think of them, and this in turn creates more stress and tendency towards perfectionism, or it can also create a complete block and avoidance of the piece of work or activity (such as a competitive sport).

It can start in childhood, with some children refusing to participate in activities if they think they won't win. This is a huge shame as they can miss out on the opportunity to try new things and share new experiences. Equally, in adulthood, being afraid to "fail" can really limit your life in terms of new adventures or encounters.

It can help to remember famous "failures" when you feel like this, and what those people achieved despite rejection or setback. People like JK Rowling, for example, whose Harry Potter manuscripts were initially rejected by multiple publishers, or Walt Disney, who was told at 22 that he was "not creative enough" and was fired from his newspaper job.

Failure is a part of life, and one that we perhaps don't share enough with others (which may be understandable, even though it would be helpful), but it is key to how we learn, so try not to fear it, and instead use every mistake and every opportunity for feedback to help shape your work to make it better.

TOP TIPS:

- Don't avoid trying new things or things you may feel are out of your comfort zone because you might not be brilliant at them or you might "fail".
- Take "good risks". This might include choosing an unfamiliar but interesting topic to study for a short module or student-led project, applying for a role that is likely to stretch you but be enjoyable, or research something that will be challenging and may not work out but will be rewarding as a process.
- View mistakes and when things go wrong as all part of the learning experience of university or life.
- If things go wrong, take time to feel upset, but then take a breath, meet a friend to moan about it, deal with it, exercise furiously, sleep on it, and try to move on, if it is not of genuine life and death significance.

3. Unrealistic expectations and time-management issues (or, "work is all-consuming")

Do you ever feel as though you haven't got enough time for all the things you need (let alone want!) to do? Do you hand work in late (or get close to doing so) on a regular basis? Do you live and breathe your thesis or academic work? Do you find it hard to switch off from all your activities, including your studies?

You may be suffering from unrealistic expectations of what you can manage and / or poor time management.

These are issues that can affect all sorts of students when juggling deadlines, having creative ideas, prepping for exams, keeping up with extracurricular or family activities, social engagements, and university events.

It is common for students to take on or sign up to loads of things, then spend their entire time rushing about yelling, 'I'm so busy! I haven't got enough time!'

Deadlines slide, the weeks race by and, before you know it, exam time's arrived and you're in a panic because you've spent too much time on non-academic activities, or not quite got the balance right on your different academic modules and workloads.

Help is at hand!

Again, time management is an issue that is well recognised by universities, and they are certainly skills that will stand you in good stead for life. This is why most institutions run time management and academic planning skills training workshops for their students. All you have to do is enquire and sign up (and actually go)!

Some universities have run "You are not your thesis" campaigns to address the risk of over-immersing yourself in academic study, and they also tackle difficulties with supervisors, low motivation, and "second-year blues", so it might be helpful to seek out advice on these topics if they are getting you down.

If you feel you can't talk to your supervisor for example, try putting it in writing, and if that doesn't work, seek out post-grad support groups locally or online for relevant advice.

TOP TIPS:

In the meantime, try these tips to get life back under control and set yourself realistic expectations:

- Take a good hard look at what you need to be doing and what you are doing because it's fun / good for your CV. Prune back a couple of activities that might be less essential to create some time. You can always do them again in the future!

- Ask for academic support from your tutor / supervisor early on, especially about planning work / prioritising modules / deadlines and so on.
- Draw up a timetable on a spreadsheet with all your deadlines / exams etc. written in so that you have a clear timeline. Then, write in when certain tasks have to be done by in preparation for meeting the final deadlines, e.g. 'read this paper in time for writing such and such essay'.
- Work with friends (if you find it helpful) to learn together, be creative together or practise together, as you'll be more likely to sit down and do the work if you have committed to do it with someone else. It can be fun too, of course.
- Schedule some treats for when you achieve something on your planner.
- Use time-management apps.
- Build in time to exercise, relax and eat healthy snacks, as well as see other people (in person!). It is so important to stay well when working and juggling your busy life!

4. Imposter syndrome

If you have ever felt like "everyone else is cleverer than me, a faster reader than me, better than me at this topic", or as though you "don't deserve to be at this university" and that you are a "fish out of water", then you may have imposter syndrome.

You are not alone.

It is really quite common to feel like you are the odd one out, and that someone is at any moment going to point out that you shouldn't be here, that there's been a mistake, and would you please just leave the course / the university etc.

You might feel like you have no idea what you're doing, and that someone is bound to notice soon. You perhaps forget that you had to go through a selection process in order to get into university, and that you have as much right to be there as anyone else, as well as the absolute ability and potential to achieve great things.

Some of our most well-known Hollywood stars have talked about how they sometimes feel like this!

Emma Stone said (in September 2017) "I sometimes feel like an imposter and think 'why do I deserve to be here?'", and Ryan Reynolds has had similar feelings, saying "to be honest, I still feel like a freckle-faced kid, faking it until I make it."

TOP TIPS:

Imposter syndrome is common, and once you know what it is, you can:

- **Acknowledge** your feelings and share them with others who you trust
- **Think about what you are good at** (give yourself a pat on the back for that!)
- **Remind yourself** that you were good enough to get where you are now
- **Stop comparing yourself** with others
- **Set yourself realistic goals** to achieve and enjoy to reinforce what you are good at and boost your confidence (ox.ac.uk)

Remember, you are *not* a fraud and you *do* deserve to be here, along with all the success that will follow.

CHAPTER 6

PERSONAL PROBLEMS

Some of the issues that affect students are related to their personal lives, including feeling homesick, worrying about their own identity, money stress, or, more commonly than you might think, struggling with their purpose in life. The good news is that universities are full of people waiting to help you with such problems, from the Students' Union and Chaplaincy to the Counselling and GP teams. Just ask them for confidential advice if you're finding it tough.

1. Homesickness

It doesn't matter where you're from or how far (or not) you are from home; students often get homesick. It's not uncommon for GPs to see homesick students whose families live less than an hour from the university and who go home at every opportunity they can. They will likely also have looked after lots of students from overseas who not only have to deal with the academic demands of university, but have to do so in a new language, culture, climate and in foreign surroundings.

TOP TIPS:

- **Try not to go home for at least the first four weeks of term** – it is very common to feel a bit displaced and lonely at first, but if you possibly can, try not to go home for at least the **first four weeks** of university term. This will allow you to settle in better, meet other students, go to events and start feeling like you belong in this new institution. Going home after that is perfectly reasonable and you shouldn't try to "push through" and not go home at all if you want to and would feel better for doing so.

- **Get involved in workshops** – many universities run workshops for homesick students to help them settle in. Some organise multiple activities to build your social networks. So, give these a try, and even if some of them are not your natural environment or make you feel a bit uncertain, some might lead to meeting a new friend, or finding out about a new activity that would otherwise have passed you by.

- **Ask your family to send small care packages** – some students like to receive parcels including favourite snacks, magazines or postcards. This might be a good idea for you as long as it doesn't make you feel worse.

- **Plan ahead** – it can be helpful to plan visits home, or visitors from home every few weeks can be fun, or even planning for the holidays if it's too far to travel during term time, of course.

- **Create a home WhatsApp group** – this can be a nice way to feel part of discussions and chat about home life, without actually being there, again as long as it doesn't make you miss them too much and isn't all-consuming.

- **Stay busy** – not locked away in your room, and make sure you meet people and get out and about, and explore your new surroundings to gradually reduce the feelings of missing home.

- If the homesickness doesn't seem to be wearing off gradually and you are feeling more down, flat or numb, even after several weeks have passed, then don't hesitate to **seek help and talk to a professional about it**; this feeling can progress to a more depressive type of episode for some people.

2. Identity (self / new / changing)

Being a young adult arriving at a new university creates a moment of real opportunity to establish your self-identity. You can create a "new you": try out a new persona, or explore your sexuality, gender, race and culture in ways that may never have been possible previously, and in an environment that is likely to be tolerant and supportive of it.

This wonderful new freedom to be yourself or curate the "new you" can also bring conflict of course, as your family, friends from home and perhaps some of your new contacts adjust (or not) to the new reality.

You no longer fit into the you-shaped hole you left behind.

It may be helpful therefore to **talk** about your thoughts and ideas, and any plans you may have to change your identity or emphasise certain aspects of it, with those people who are most likely to be affected *prior* to changes occurring (if you can).

Break it to them gently if possible.

TOP TIPS:

Other tips for establishing a new you include:

- Drop hints about it and try to remember that just because it feels right for you, it may not feel right yet for everyone who loves you (even if it should).

- If your appearance has changed, can you share photos before they see you in person, or at least let them know in advance?

- If your politics or values have shifted, try to have gentle conversations around the topic, or accept that you might have to avoid it on occasion to keep the peace, if your views are unlikely to be shared.

- If you have become vegan, don't assume that others have to cook to your tastes and choices – be prepared to help out by offering to bring your own food initially.

- It won't always be easy but try to **be considerate about how you reveal the new you,** and of the impact it might have on relationships and established views / politics / religious choices. Your choices may be seen as a criticism of another person's life choices, even if that's not how it's meant, and being aware of this can allow for a diplomatic approach where possible.

Many GPs will unfortunately have witnessed and supported students though dreadful breakdowns in family relations as they established their new identities or lifestyles in direct conflict with their parents' beliefs or understanding. The students were absolutely not at fault, and prior discussion might not have changed the parents' feelings or the overall outcomes, but it is always worth trying to talk things through in life.

They will sadly also have known students to take their own lives when they felt unable to be themselves or live true to their sexuality or beliefs, and such heart breaking events might have been avoided (we will never know) if the young person had felt accepted and supported by society, their community or their family. If you recognise this conflict in yourself, please do talk to the university's support staff, who are absolutely committed to *helping you to be you*.

3. Lack of purpose or reason for being, also known as an "existential crisis"

Interestingly, GPs will see many students over the years who are deeply troubled by their lack of purpose in life, their feeling that the world seems pointless, or their belief that life is a charade or has no meaning for them.

Clearly there can be close links with depression in some of these beliefs and feelings, but often those young people will have thought about the meaning of life for many months or years, and have not been able to find a meaning for themselves.

They have then become quite low and, in some cases, thought about ending their lives because of this lack of purpose or reason for living, but for them suicide seems a rational decision, made after prolonged deliberation and consideration of their future options.

Lack of purpose or direction can actually be one of the most serious risks to young people's mental health so you should definitely seek support if this feels like you.

Real-life example

Damon was a 20-year-old second-year student when he saw the counselling service. He seemed very flat, and his manner was subdued. His flatmates had encouraged him to come, and were in the waiting room. They had become increasingly concerned about his comments, which were along the lines of 'What's the point? There's no reason for me to be here. I might as well not be.' He had not been enjoying his course, and couldn't see where it might take him. He had no idea what he wanted to do with his life and was beginning to think that he had no purpose or reason for carrying on.

The counsellor listened, and explained that it was not uncommon for young adults to still be looking for their purpose in life and that sometimes it could take a few years to settle on a reason for being, a reason to get up every day and go to work, volunteer, or be active in the world. The counsellor suggested that Damon speak to the careers service for some new ideas about work opportunities or experience, as well as taking time to think about doing something for others that might give him a renewed sense of achievement, such as through a local kids' charity, or at a homeless or animal shelter.

They agreed to keep talking and see what other ideas they could come up with that might help him to rediscover his motivation and commitment to "keep going while seeing where life took him".

Are you having an existential crisis or struggling to feel a sense of purpose?

It's not so much "I'm so hopeless, I feel so awful, things will never get better, what's the point in carrying on?" but more:

"Life is pointless, there doesn't seem to be any greater purpose or reason for me to be here, I'm not contributing anything useful, what's the point in carrying on?"

Solutions and strategies

If you recognise the latter sentiments, then yes, you may well be struggling with your reason for living – although if you are having either of these conversations with yourself, you should certainly talk to a health and wellbeing expert such as a GP, counsellor, psychologist or other student support professional soon in order to share your emotions and find ways to feel better.

But you are not alone, and such feelings have even been given the name "quarter-life crisis" – though this seems a little dismissive of what can present as very serious psychological distress, and which professionals are always happy to talk through with any struggling student.

It can take time, but with support, counselling, or therapy, young adults can come through what is a questioning and often confusing period and emerge the other side with a new perspective on their purpose in life (which may not yet be clearly defined, but which will evolve and take shape with the coming years).

Try This:

Goal Setting

This can be useful as a technique if you've lost your way. Setting goals, even just bite-sized "mini goals", can give you a sense of purpose when you are feeling lost. These might include anything from having a daily shower (if you've been feeling really low), to meeting a friend for coffee, or reading two chapters of a book.

Setting goals is recognised to improve what psychologists call "self-agency", defined as "the ability to have control over your actions", or your "free will" – essentially, control over your life's direction and choices.

If you set yourself goals, and then choose to engage and achieve them, this will positively feedback and make you feel better about yourself, as well as underlining the fact that you are in charge of what you do, and have that control and direction over your life.

Examples

1. If you set your goal as walking round the block every day, and you do this, and slowly you start to feel better (for being outside, for seeing other people in passing, for getting the exercise), then you can give yourself a pat on the back after a couple of weeks, and know that you can do this one thing. Next time you might then try to walk a little further, through a park, or to the shops.

2. Another goal, if you are feeling very lost and low in your emotions, might be to go online and book a counselling or GP appointment to talk about how you're feeling. Ask someone to help you if it feels overwhelming but you would like to go, and maybe take a friend or family member with you. The goal after that may then be to keep going back for follow-up appointments, or to start therapy of course.

It is important to set *realistic* goals; you don't want to set yourself up to fail, and it's good to make the goals something you can measure ("I will read two chapters", "I will book an appointment") so you know you have achieved them.

Don't give up if things don't go well immediately, but stick with those goals and you will feel so much better when you do achieve them.

4. Financial Problems

Finances definitely cause worries for students (and their families) at university, but it's not just the tuition fees that cause concerns; the cost of daily living, rent, food, clothes, and any treats such as holidays etc. create a significant amount of stress. This financial stress is recognised as being really important for students, and there are now some brilliant websites and resources to help you with what may seem like boring tasks (like budgeting), but might literally save you thousands in cash (as well as your sanity) over the next few years!

TOP TIPS:

- **Download free budget spreadsheets** (at savethestudent. org) to fill in your "income" (loan, salary from part-time jobs, savings, monetary gifts at birthday and Christmas).
- **Write down everything you spend**, so that you can see if it balances out. It can be eye-opening to see how much those lattes and lunches add up to!

- **Set monthly and yearly smart goals for yourself** (find downloadable guides at Blackbullion.com).
- **Research the various types of student bank accounts available** – some of them even include deals and incentives (moneysavingexpert.com).
- **Get an overdraft** on your bank account if possible (but be careful not to abuse it, as this can make matters worse).

Such websites also have great top tips for saving on daily expenses, such as:

- **Making your own lunches** and taking them with you
- **Cycling** instead of taking public transport
- **Doing surveys and market research** for cash and tokens at the university
- **Getting cheap haircuts** by being the trainee hairdresser's guinea pig
- **Getting discount, loyalty and membership cards** wherever possible (Blackbullion.com)
- **Shopping the reduced sections** in shops and supermarkets

There are also huge numbers of apps to help save you money – again check out savethestudent.org and blackbullion.com for more advice.

What next for your financial planning?

As with many challenges, the key is to plan ahead, not bury your head in the sand, and think about possible ways to save money that suit your life, but feel realistic. You are probably not going to be able to get a part-time job if you are doing a full-time course, but you could work in the holidays perhaps, to earn some cash for the year ahead.

Or how about babysitting for one of your lecturers, dog walking at weekends for cash, and so on?

Feeling financially flat?

Don't hide away!

If you are feeling the financial stress, don't shut yourself away and stop socialising to "save money" as this will just make you feel worse. Find activities that are free or very cheap, go running instead of to a gym, and stay active and connected to others, while using the savings tips mentioned on the websites above.

In summary

Some of these personal or financial problems can feel all too much sometimes, and really make everyday life a struggle. By setting yourself small, achievable goals it may be possible to manage and overcome the barriers you face, while making yourself feel better for doing so. You may need professional support, especially if the problems are making you feel very flat or lost, but the help is out there – you just need to ask. These issues are common, and can be dealt with, but everyone needs a helping hand sometimes.

CHAPTER 7

"TRANSITION BLUES"

Going to university, travelling for the holidays or field trips, moving accommodation, studying abroad, placements, leaving university for the workplace, or moving onto further academic studies ... for students, the change is constant and the transitions never-ending.

It's not surprising that some students get "transition blues", ranging from post-travelling / gap year blues to graduation blues, or even transition-related depression in the more severe cases.

That feeling of being dislocated, of not quite fitting, that everyone else knows what's going on except you, or that you have experienced something that no one else can quite understand – these are all common feelings in the different scenarios and circumstances mentioned above. Going through these experiences with another person can really bond you together, but it can also mean that you feel that only *they* can truly understand your situation. This is thankfully *not* the case.

Student Minds, the mental health charity, also has some brilliant resources to help with transitions, which look at what to expect and how to cope with change, at different stages of life.

TOP TIPS:

• Share your feelings

You are not alone in feeling disconnected or different at university, although it may be for reasons that differ from someone else's feelings, so remember to talk to other students. *Share* the feelings you are having, even if they haven't shared exactly the same experience, as they are likely to understand and empathise, despite the fact that their situation involved being in industry, for example, rather than Paris for a year.

• Keep busy

While it will be natural to reflect back on a happy experience and miss the people or places that made it special, it is important to rediscover a sense of purpose and drive for where you are and what you are doing *now*. For example, if you have graduated from university and are job hunting, but feeling down that your student days are behind you, then focus your mind on what you need to be doing to polish your CV, test your interview skills, build up work experience, or do some volunteering etc., while occasionally allowing yourself a quick look at photos of your best uni days. It's important to try not to wallow in them, however, or become morose that they are over, as the past is a sad and unproductive place to live. You have a fantastic future ahead of you, using your brilliant uni experience to create it!

• Create new networks

When you're at school, you might imagine that school friends will be the only friends you will ever need. Then, of course, university comes along and you meet a whole new set of people, which, over the years, you hone down to a key tribe of "uni friends".

However, the process happens again as you move on into the workplace, then again if you meet your "soul mate", if and when you have kids, when you join a sports team or have a particular hobby and so on, so that in fact, as life goes on, you will have *several* sets of supportive, reliable friends; networks that you call on or spend time with depending on your mood or situation, but who are more or less closely present over the years.

So, take these moments of **transition** as opportunities to create new networks, meet new people, test out new friendships or hobbies or interests, not ignoring your old friends of course, but adding to your spider's web of interconnections, without necessarily knowing if those new connections will last or lead to interesting future possibilities.

• Try something new (and possibly scary!)

Coping with change is one of life's hardest challenges, and most people don't like it. But if you can, try to see it as an **opportunity** wherever possible rather than as a threat or worry.

Look for the positives, say yes to things that might make you a little nervous but will test you too, such as job opportunities in unknown locations, or openings in organisations you might not have previously considered, or trying a new activity or team sport. Without being foolhardy or engaging in overly risky behaviour, assess the challenge and talk it through with others, plan for it, then make the leap, and do something that **stretches** you.

Try This:

Learned Optimism

Learned optimism is the idea of taking a pessimistic view of an experience and turning it into an optimistic view. It was defined by Martin Seligman in 1990 in his book *Learned Optimism*, and is part of the Positive Psychology approach.

It is about viewing difficult situations as *unlucky setbacks*, not personal slights and *not permanent* in their effect. It's about cultivating a positive outlook, being a "glass half full" kind of person. The theory is that we can develop this, we are not just *born* a pessimist or optimist.

In some ways, learned optimism is the opposite of "learned helplessness" (see the frog metaphor below), where, as things get harder, you slowly give up.

As life gets tougher, we can sometimes feel like quitting. This is where learned optimism may be a helpful technique, allowing you to view the difficult situation through a different lens, if possible.

Cognitive behavioural approaches with a therapist use this technique for conditions such as depression.

You can learn approaches such as:

- Taking time to be **grateful** for the good things in your life
- **Actively** stop yourself when you feel yourself starting to ruminate about the bad things
- **Using positive language** and phrases
- **Surrounding yourself** with positive people

Watch Out For Learned Helplessness – The Frog Metaphor

The often-used metaphor is of the frog and a saucepan of boiling water. They say that if you put a frog in boiling water, it will, of course, jump out immediately, but that if you put it into cold water then heat it up gradually, it won't notice and will eventually die (please don't try this at home!).

The latter behaviour is essentially an example of learned helplessness.

In other words, if we are immersed in a constantly challenging situation, we may be more likely to give up than if we arrive fresh to it, and can fight back and have the energy to get ourselves out of it. This is sometimes seen with toxic relationships, which can develop over time, and lead people to stay in a difficult situation when they have lost the energy or belief that they can and should leave. Students are as likely as anyone else to have relationships which are unpleasant, co-dependent or bad for them in another way, and in the worst cases are violent or abusive, so this learned helplessness is sometimes seen at university and must not be ignored.

The aim of learned optimism is to improve outlook and, in the longer term, your health, as optimists have better health than pessimists, and less depression, according to Seligman. It is a useful skill, though clearly not enough in itself to cope with very difficult or challenging relationships or other scenarios, but can be helpful for dealing with change and new challenges in life such as transition.

In summary

Transition and change are hard for most people, but it is up to you whether you view these times as threats or opportunities. By looking at such moments positively and embracing the possibilities, you will likely pass through them more successfully as well as giving yourself a better shot at good physical and mental health.

CHAPTER 8

IN SUMMARY

So, throughout the course of this book, we've discovered:

- That life, and university in particular, can be complicated and challenging
- That life changes constantly and transition is tricky
- That it takes time to find our purpose in life
- That pressures will come from academic work, relationships, financial hardship and our (sometimes unrealistic) expectations of ourselves, and the notions that others have of who we are and what we should be
- That there are plenty of ways to make new friends and meet people
- That we can be pretty tough on ourselves; that we think we are not good enough or undeserving of success, which isn't always helpful
- But that there are many ways to manage these difficulties, if we can simply take a moment to think about what is happening around us and what we can do to tackle the situation

You will hopefully have identified some of the specific problems you are facing and read the suggested tips, solutions or strategies to address them, or at least know when and where to get help if you need support to do this.

You may be feeling inspired to develop your growth mindset (stretch yourself), set some goals, have conversations with yourself or try some learned optimism, all of which are really useful lifelong skills to have in your **toolkit of resourcefulness**.

And one final reassuring truth to think about, when despair hits, or you feel frustrated by conflict or unsure how to move forwards:

"This too shall pass"

It's an ancient saying, around for centuries, and used by Abraham Lincoln among others, allegedly, to acknowledge that everything is temporary.

Sometimes we all need help to remember that bad times will pass, and that, although tragic things happen, we can cope even when we feel like we can't. Everything is a phase.

Life will bring good phases and bad phases, and *both* will end, so when life is tough it can be helpful to remind ourselves that the tough times are temporary.

Or as Winston Churchill once said, "If you're going through hell, keep going".

What does that mean for you?

Sometimes, when you're "going through hell", it can feel never-ending, relentlessly depressing and like every day is a chore.

Believe it or not, most people have known that feeling at some point in their lives, and with age and experience you usually learn that such dreadful times pass to some extent (albeit maybe not completely), that the pain lessens and life moves forwards–despite how hard this might seem when you've got your whole life ahead of you.

How do I keep going?

Humans are extraordinarily resilient to trauma, and distress, so it may help to try to remember, when things feel unendingly awful, that they *will* get better, and you may just need to get through a day (or even an hour) at a time, as well as **talk** about how you are feeling, get **professional** support, take **comfort** from other humans (or pets), and try to hold onto a shred of **hope** as you push through the days. Don't give up; reach out.

Hopefully this book has offered the reassurance that you are not alone, the knowledge that there are things that you can do and that your future is very much in your control, and that it will have inspired you to get there more happily and feeling healthier.

If you need extra support, that is completely normal and understandable; we are all human, we all go through difficult times, and we all need a helping hand sometimes.

University is a place to learn – and not just academically, but also about life and how to manage when the going gets tough.

Universities are filled with helpful souls whose jobs involve supporting students, so reach out and ask if you need help, or get a friend or family member to help you onto that first step of the path, if you feel unable to do it alone.

Either is fine, but **do** reach out, please don't suffer in silence.

You *can* do this. It *can* get better.

CHAPTER 9

WHERE CAN I FIND OUT MORE?

TED talks

- Carol Dweck – "The Power of Believing That You Can Improve"
- Russell Foster – "Why Do We Sleep?"
- Sarah Jayne Blakemore – "The Mysterious Workings of the Adolescent Brain"
- Dominique Thompson – "What I Learnt from 78000 GP Consultations with University Students"
- Thomas Curran – "Our Dangerous Obsession with Perfectionism Is Getting Worse"

FODMAP diet for irritable bowel syndrome

https://www.theibsnetwork.org/diet/fodmaps/

Money advice

www.blackbullion.com
www.savethestudent.org

Perfectionism

https://www.cci.health.wa.gov.au/Resources/Looking-After-Yourself/Perfectionism
https://ray.yorksj.ac.uk/id/eprint/2966/1/Perfectionism%20fact%20sheet.pdf

Apps

- *Student Health App* – for all health matters
- *CBT-I apps* – for insomnia
- *distrACT* – for self-harm
- Headspace (for mindfulness)
- SAM app (for anxiety)

Websites

- NHS support **www.nhs.uk**
- The Mix **www.themix.org.uk**
- Mind **www.mind.org.uk** or call **0300 123 3393**
- Moodgym (for CBT skills) **www.moodgym.com.au**
- Student Minds (the UK national student mental health charity) **www.studentminds.org.uk**
- Drug info **www.talktofrank.com**
- Alcohol info **www.drinkaware.co.uk**
- Addiction **www.addaction.org.uk**
- Gambling and gaming **www.gamequitters.com** and **www.gamanon.org.uk**
- Eating issues **www.network-ed.org.uk**
- ADHD **www.adhdfoundation.org.uk**
- Aspergers **www.autism.org.uk**
- Gender issues **www.mermaidsuk.org.uk**
- LGBT+ **www.stonewall.org.uk**

YouTube

Pooky Knightsmith on Mental Health videos

REFERENCES

Bembenutty, H. (2011). *Academic delay of gratification and academic achievement.* [online] Ssrlsite.files.wordpress.com. Available at: https://ssrlsite.files.wordpress.com/2018/01/ bembenutty-2011-academic-delay-of-grat-and-academic-achievement.pdf [Accessed 2 Jan. 2019].

Blackwell, L., Trzesniewski, K. and Dweck, C. (2007). Implicit Theories of Intelligence Predict Achievement Across an Adolescent Transition: A Longitudinal Study and an Intervention. *Child Development,* [online] 78(1), pp.246–63. Available at: https://www.mtoliveboe.org/cmsAdmin/ uploads/blackwell-theories-of-intelligence-child-dev-2007.pdf. [Accessed 22 Dec. 2018].

Carey, B. (2015). *How We Learn.* New York, NY: Random House.

Curran, T. and Hill, A. (2017). Perfectionism is increasing over time: A meta-analysis of birth cohort differences from 1989 to 2016. *Psychological Bulletin.* [online] Available at: https://www.ncbi.nlm.nih.gov/pubmed/29283599 [Accessed 31 Dec. 2018].

Duckworth, A. (2016). *Grit.* London Vermillion.

Dweck, C. and Leggett, E. (1988). A social cognitive approach to motivation and personality. *Psychological Review,* [online] 95(2), pp.256–73. Available at: http://citeseerx.ist.psu.edu/viewdoc/ download?doi=10.1.1.583.9142&rep=rep1&type=pdf.

HEPI. (2018). *Most students think taking illegal drugs causes problems for users as well as society and want their universities to take a tougher stance – HEPI.* [online] Available at: https://www.hepi.ac.uk/2018/06/12/students-think-taking-illegal-drugs-causes-problems-users-well-society-want-universities-take-tougher-stance/ [Accessed 31 Dec. 2018].

Hystad, S., Eid, J., Laberg, J., Johnsen, B. and Bartone, P. (2009). Academic Stress and Health: Exploring the Moderating Role of Personality Hardiness. *Scandinavian Journal of Educational Research*, [online] 53(5), pp.421–29. Available at: https://www.tandfonline.com/doi/abs/10.1080/00313830903180349?journalCode=csje20 [Accessed 2 Jan. 2019].

Jose, P., Ryan, N. and Pryor, J. (2012). Does Social Connectedness Promote a Greater Sense of Well-Being in Adolescence Over Time?. *Journal of Research on Adolescence*, 22(2), pp.235–51.

Medlineplus.gov. (n.d.). *Tips for Getting A Good Night's Sleep | NIH MedlinePlus the Magazine.* [online] Available at: https://medlineplus.gov/magazine/issues/summer15/articles/summer15pg22.html [Accessed 3 Jan. 2019].

Mind.org.uk. (2019). **Five ways to wellbeing | Mind, the mental health charity – help for mental health problems.** [online] Available at: https://www.mind.org.uk/workplace/mental-health-at-work/taking-care-of-yourself/five-ways-to-wellbeing/ [Accessed 19 Apr. 2019].

NCISH. (2017). *Suicide by children and young people – NCISH.* [online] Available at: https://sites.manchester.ac.uk/ncish/reports/suicide-by-children-and-young-people/ [Accessed 31 Dec. 2018].

NCISH. (2018). *Annual report 2018: England, Northern Ireland, Scotland and Wales – NCISH.* [online] Available at: https://sites.manchester.ac.uk/ncish/reports/annual-report-2018-

england-northern-ireland-scotland-and-wales/ [Accessed 31 Dec. 2018].

Neff, K. (2018). *Self-Compassion.* [online] Self-Compassion. Available at: https://self-compassion.org [Accessed 2 Jan. 2019].

Oppong, T. (2018). *The Theory of "Grit" as a Predictor of Success in Life.* [online] Medium. Available at: https://medium.com/personal-growth/the-theory-of-grit-as-a-predictor-of-success-in-life-24274ceec46 [Accessed 2 Jan. 2019].

Ox.ac.uk. (n.d.). *Expectations, Transitions and Overcoming Imposter Syndrome.* [online] Available at: https://www.ox.ac.uk/sites/files/oxford/field/field_document/Expectation%2C%20Transitions%20and%20Overcoming%20Imposter%20Syndrome.pdf [Accessed 2 Jan. 2019].

Rasch, D. (2018). *The Procrastination Wheel of Suffering: Part Five – Anxiety, Deadlines and Binge Writing.* [online] David Rasch PhD. Available at: https://davidraschphd.wordpress.com/2018/05/02/the-procrastination-wheel-of-suffering-part-five-anxiety-deadlines-and-binge-writing/ [Accessed 2 Jan. 2019].

SC, K. (1979). *Stressful life events, personality, and health: an inquiry into hardiness. – PubMed – NCBI.* [online] Ncbi.nlm.nih.gov. Available at: https://www.ncbi.nlm.nih.gov/pubmed/458548 [Accessed 2 Jan. 2019].

Seligman, M. (1990). *Learned optimism.* New York, NY: Knopf.

Thompson, D. (2018). *What I learnt from 78,000 GP consultations with university students | Dominique Thompson | TEDxBath.* [online] YouTube. Available at: https://www.youtube.com/watch?v=gt-ToFPHCkI [Accessed 31 Dec. 2018].

Van Edwards, V. (2018). *Learn How to Make Friends As An Adult Using These 5 Steps.* [online] Science of People. Available at: https://www.scienceofpeople.com/how-to-make-friends/ [Accessed 3 Jan. 2019].

Walker, M. (2017). *Why we sleep.* London: Allen Lane.

Www2.open.ac.uk. (2018). *Active reading – Skills for OU Study – Open University.* [online] Available at: http://www2.open.ac.uk/students/skillsforstudy/active-reading.php [Accessed 2 Jan. 2019].

If you found this book interesting ...
why not read these next?

Doing Single Well

**A Guide to Living, Loving and
Dating without compromise**

Doing Single Well will help you find fulfilment
in your single life, and if you want a partner,
to wait for one who is right for you.

Body Image Problems
& Body Dysmorphic Disorder

The Definitive Treatment and Recovery Approach

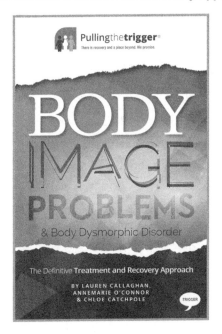

This unique and inspiring book provides simple yet highly
effective self-help methods to help you overcome your body
image concerns and Body Dysmorphic Disorder (BDD).

the *Shaw* mind
FOUNDATION

Creating hope for children,
adults and families

Sign up to our charity, The Shaw Mind Foundation

www.shawmindfoundation.org

and keep in touch with us; we would love to hear
from you.

*Our goal is to make help and support available for every
single person in society, from all walks of life.
We will never stop offering hope. These are our promises.*

TRIGGER™

The mental health & wellbeing publisher

www.triggerpublishing.com

Trigger is a publishing house devoted to opening conversations about mental health. We tell the stories of people who have suffered from mental illnesses and recovered, so that others may learn from them.

Adam Shaw is a worldwide mental health advocate and philanthropist. Now in recovery from mental health issues, he is committed to helping others suffering from debilitating mental health issues through the global charity he co-founded, The Shaw Mind Foundation. www.shawmindfoundation.org

Lauren Callaghan (CPsychol, PGDipClinPsych, PgCert, MA (hons), LLB (hons), BA), born and educated in New Zealand, is an innovative industry-leading psychologist based in London, United Kingdom. Lauren has worked with children and young people, and their families, in a number of clinical settings providing evidence based treatments for a range of illnesses, including anxiety and obsessional problems. She was a psychologist at the specialist national treatment centres for severe obsessional problems in the UK and is renowned as an expert in the field of mental health, recognised for diagnosing and successfully treating OCD and anxiety related illnesses in particular. In addition to appearing as a treating clinician in the critically acclaimed and BAFTA award-winning documentary *Bedlam*, Lauren is a frequent guest speaker on mental health conditions in the media and at academic conferences. Lauren also acts as a guest lecturer and honorary researcher at the Institute of Psychiatry Kings College, UCL.

Please visit the link below:
www.triggerpublishing.com

Join us and follow us ...

@triggerpub
@Shaw_Mind

Search for us on Facebook